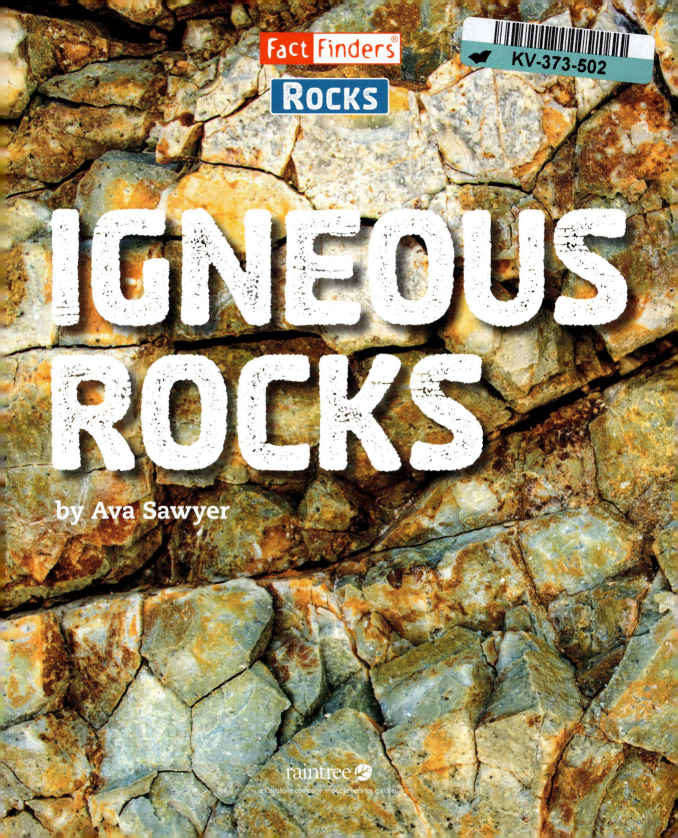

Fact Finders®

Rocks

IGNEOUS ROCKS

by Ava Sawyer

raintree

a Capstone company — publishers for children

Raintree is an imprint of Capstone Global Library Limited, a company incorporated in England and Wales having its registered office at 264 Banbury Road, Oxford, OX2 7DY – Registered company number: 6695582

www.raintree.co.uk
myorders@raintree.co.uk

Edited by Nikki Potts
Designed by Sarah Bennett
Original illustrations © Capstone Global Library Limited 2019
Picture research by Jo Miller
Production by Laura Manthe
Originated by Capstone Global Library Ltd
Printed and bound in India

ISBN 978 1 4747 6017 1 (hardback)
22 21 20 19 18
10 9 8 7 6 5 4 3 2 1

ISBN 978 1 4747 6025 6 (paperback)
23 22 21 20 19
10 9 8 7 6 5 4 3 2 1

British Library Cataloguing in Publication Data
A full catalogue record for this book is available from the British Library.

Acknowledgements
We would like to thank the following for permission to reproduce photographs: Alamy: Siim Sepp, 10 (middle bottom); Dreamstime: Ciolca, 27, Stefano Valeri, 12; Getty Images: Steve and Donna O'Meara, 26; Science Source: Dirk Wiersma, 19, Spencer Sutton, 11; Shutterstock: Adboabdalla, 29 (bottom), AlanMorris, 8 (bottom), Aleksandr Pobedimskiy, 13 (top), Alexey Stiop, 15, Darryl Brooks, 28 (right), DarwelShots, 4, Ellen Bronstayn, 6, Everett Historical, 25, gaa166, cover, Gherzak, 10 (middle), Gudjon E. Olafsson, 8 (middle bottom), Hale Kell, 2-3, Kicky_princess, 22 (top left), Layouts Studios, 10 (top), Lucy Brown - loca4motion, 5, Mariusz S. Jurgielewicz, 22 (bottom), MH Anderson Photography, 21, Michael Vokits, 18 (bottom), paleontologist natural, 23 (bottom), Peter Etchells, 28 (left), Sakdinon Kadchiangsaen, 14, Tarzhanova, 29 (middle), Tedrique, 18 (top), Terence Mendoza, 8 (top), torook, 29 (top), Tyler Boyes, 13 (bottom), 20 (left), 20 (middle), 22 (top right), 23 (top), vagabond54, 24, vvoe, 8 (middle top), 20 (right), Wead, 17, Wildnerdpix, 9, Willyam Bradberry, 7; Wikimedia: M. Hollunder, 10 (bottom) **Design Elements:** Shutterstock: Alted Studio, AnVdErGiA

Every effort has been made to contact copyright holders of material reproduced in this book. Any omissions will be rectified in subsequent printings if notice is given to the publisher.

All the internet addresses (URLs) given in this book were valid at the time of going to press. However, due to the dynamic nature of the internet, some addresses may have changed, or sites may have changed or ceased to exist since publication. While the author and publisher regret any inconvenience this may cause readers, no responsibility for any such changes can be accepted by either the author or the publisher.

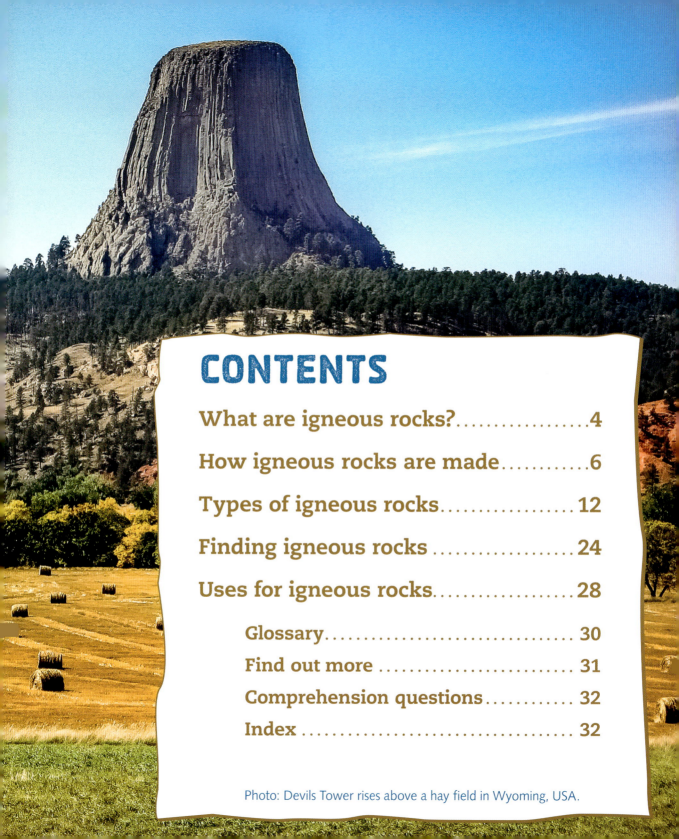

CONTENTS

Photo: Devils Tower rises above a hay field in Wyoming, USA.

CHAPTER 1

WHAT ARE IGNEOUS ROCKS?

A trickle of melted rock creeps down the side of a volcano. On top of the red-hot rock, a grey crust of cooling rock forms. A fountain of liquid rock spews out of another volcano and lights up the night sky. A wide river of fire flows down the mountainside, destroying everything in its path. From another volcano, a huge grey cloud spews forth. The cloud covers hundreds of square kilometres of land with a thick coating of ash and rock. All of these volcanoes are "factories" that create igneous rock.

Mount Sinabung in Sumatra, Indonesia

Igneous rocks form when molten rock cools. Molten rock generally comes from volcanic activity and is often called lava or magma. The word *igneous* means "made from fire or heat".

Igneous rocks are made up of at least two types of materials called minerals. Minerals are made up of atoms that are arranged in rows and columns that form **crystals**. Some igneous rocks are made up of more than just two minerals. Granite, for example, is made up of the minerals mica, feldspar, amphibole and quartz.

Lava erupts from the Fuego volcano near Antigua, Guatemala in Central America.

FACT

Igneous rocks never contain **fossils**. Fossils are the remains or impressions of prehistoric plants and animals. Because igneous rocks are made from extremely hot molten magma and lava, there is no way they could contain fossils. The plants and animals would be destroyed in the molten rock before fossils could be formed.

crystal solid substance having a regular pattern of many flat surfaces

fossil remains of an ancient plant or animal that have hardened into rock; also the preserved tracks or outline of an ancient organism

CHAPTER 2

HOW IGNEOUS ROCKS ARE MADE

Earth has three main parts. The outer part is called the crust. The mantle is found underneath the crust. The third part is underneath the mantle and is called the core.

The mantle is a very hot place where solid rock turns to molten rock called magma. There are many places in Earth's crust that contain cracks and breaks, which are often called faults or fissures. At these locations, the magma starts to seep up from the mantle to the surface of the crust. Not all magma comes from the mantle, though. In some places, such as **subduction zones**, material in the crust melts and forms magma chambers closer to Earth's surface.

PARTS OF EARTH

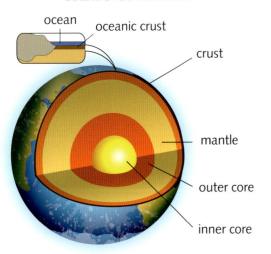

ocean

oceanic crust

crust

mantle

outer core

inner core

FACT

Earth's crust is broken into huge pieces called **tectonic plates**. There are seven major tectonic plates. The plates are named after the continents or bodies of water they carry.

subduction zone place where the edge of one tectonic plate sinks beneath another

tectonic plate gigantic slab of Earth's crust that moves around on magma

When magma rises to Earth's surface, it becomes known as lava. Once it reaches the surface, the lava does not stay liquid for long. The lava cools and hardens into a rock – igneous rock. When the igneous rocks and other materials continue to build up, a volcano is formed.

Igneous rocks can form on the dry land of the continental crust. They can also form on the seabed at the bottom of the oceanic crust. For example, all of the Hawaiian Islands are made up of igneous rocks that formed from underwater volcanoes. The volcanoes started on the ocean floor and grew as a result of millions of years of eruptions. Many types of igneous rocks can be found on these islands, including basalt, obsidian and pumice.

Hot lava flows over cooled, hardened lava in Hawaii, USA.

TYPES OF LAVA

Lava has two basic forms, lava flows and **pyroclastics**. Which form the lava takes depends on how runny or how thick and sticky the magma is. Hot lava tends to be thin and runny, but as it cools, it gets thicker and slower. There are four basic types of lava flows that cool to form **basalts** – pahoehoe, a'a, pillow lava and columnar lava.

Pahoehoe is the first type of lava to erupt from volcanoes such as those in Hawaii. It is smooth lava that cools to form various shapes such as ropes. Sometimes the outside of pahoehoe cools to form a hollow lava tube. Red-hot lava flows inside the hollow tube.

A'a lava follows pahoehoe. A'a is a cooler lava and therefore much thicker. As it flows, it cracks and breaks into chunks. These chunks pile upwards and then tumble forwards.

TYPES OF LAVA FLOW

pahoehoe

a'a

pillow

columnar

....

pyroclastic magma containing large amounts of gas that blasts out of a volcano in clouds of ash and rock

basalt hard, dark rock made from cooled lava

Pillow lava forms when lava spills out underwater or flows into water. For example, pillow lava is created when lava flows in Hawaii spill over the sea cliffs into the ocean. Pillow lavas form spheres or tube shapes.

Columnar lava can form in lava that flows out like a sheet. When a sheet of thick lava cools, it shrinks and cracks into long vertical columns. One type of columnar lava, called columnar jointed lava, makes spectacular shapes. The Giant's Causeway in Northern Ireland and Devils Tower in the United States are famous examples of columnar jointed lava.

pillow lava formation on the Green Gardens Trail in Gros Morne National Park in Newfoundland, Canada

Pyroclastics form from thick, sticky lava that contains large amounts of gas. The gas causes the lava to explode out of a volcano. The blast breaks the lava into small pieces. The smallest pyroclastic pieces are ash. Ash is like a fine powder that blows out in the clouds. Lapili are somewhat larger pieces of lava, ranging in size from the size of a peanut to the size of a walnut.

The largest pyroclastics are blocks and bombs. Blocks are square or rectangular pieces of lava. Bombs are round or tube-shaped, and they are often twisted. The magma is still hot and able to mould into a different shape when it surfaces. As it spins, the lava develops a twist.

TYPES OF PYROCLASTICS

ash

lapili

block

bomb

ROCK CYCLE

Over time, igneous rocks made from cooled lava are broken down into sediments. These sediments can be pressed or cemented together to form sedimentary rock. If heat and pressure are applied to the rock, it will turn into metamorphic rock. Later, if even greater heat is applied, the rock will turn back into magma. Then the rock cycle starts again.

Sedimentary rocks don't have to turn directly into metamorphic rocks. They could be melted into magma and then turned into igneous rocks. Metamorphic rocks can also be broken down into tiny pieces and eventually form sedimentary rocks. This is another example of how the rock cycle works.

The only thing that doesn't change during the rock cycle is what happens to magma. Magma cannot turn directly into sedimentary rock or metamorphic rock. Magma can only turn directly into igneous rock.

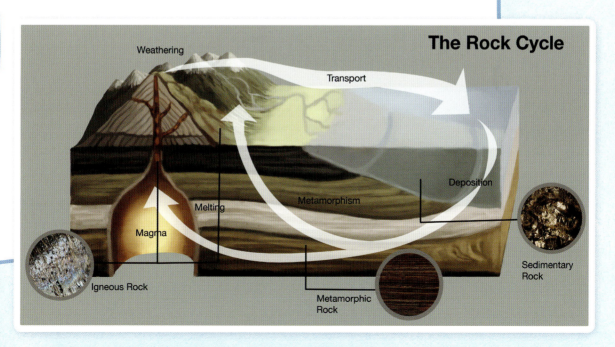

The Rock Cycle

Weathering

Transport

Deposition

Metamorphism

Melting

Magma

Igneous Rock

Metamorphic Rock

Sedimentary Rock

CHAPTER 3

TYPES OF IGNEOUS ROCKS

There are two types of igneous rocks based on where they form. They are intrusive and extrusive. Igneous rock that forms underground from cooling magma is intrusive rock. Igneous rock that forms above ground from cooling lava is extrusive rock. The prefixes are the key to remembering the difference. *In-* means "inside". *Ex-* means "outside". Extrusive rock is also known as volcanic rock. Intrusive rock is also known as plutonic rock.

The rock formations at Black Cuillin Ridge in Scotland are remnants of an old volcano.

The size of the crystals in an igneous rock is related to how fast the rock was formed. The magma cools slowly for an intrusive rock, and large crystals are formed. The lava cools quickly for an extrusive rock, and smaller crystals are formed.

Granite is a common intrusive igneous rock. It has large crystals and can be found in many colours such as white, pink and grey. The colours come from the various minerals that make up granite. This rock usually includes different amounts of mica, amphibole, feldspar and quartz.

Gabbro is another common intrusive igneous rock. This rock is normally very dark in colour. It can be a solid dark grey, or sometimes it has more of a salt-and-pepper appearance. Gabbro's dark colour comes from minerals such as plagioclase, feldspar and pyroxene. Granite and gabbro have the same texture, but they are different rocks because of the minerals inside them.

granite

gabbro

Basalt is an extrusive rock commonly found in volcanic areas. The grain size of basalt is fine, which means the crystals are so small they can barely be seen without a magnifying glass. Some samples of basalt are dark in colour and almost black. Others are lighter grey. Basalt and gabbro have the same minerals, but basalt is fine grained and gabbro is coarse grained.

basalt

MINERALS

Minerals are non-living solids that are found in rocks and soil. They are made of elements. There are 92 chemical elements found in nature. Elements are made up of tiny particles called atoms. Each element is made of only one type of atom. Atoms of one element combine in various ways with the atoms of another to create different minerals. Igneous rocks are made of two or more minerals.

Magma that rises to Earth's surface contains various mixes of minerals. Even though there are around 3,000 minerals, most are rare. Earth's rocks are mainly made up of about 100 minerals, but most igneous rocks are mostly made up of only 8 minerals.

basalt rocks in Iceland

GROUPING IGNEOUS ROCKS

Another way **geologists** group igneous rocks is based on the **composition** of the rocks – either their chemistry or the minerals that make them up. Composition is important because it tells geologists where the magma came from in Earth and how the rock changed with time.

The most common way to group igneous rocks is by the minerals that make them up. A method of ranking these minerals is called Bowen's reaction series. It shows how minerals crystallize as magma cools and turns into igneous rock. The rocks in this series are grouped by the temperatures at which they formed and by the type of magma the rocks formed from. The rocks are divided into four types of magma – mafic, intermediate, felsic and ultramafic. In addition to having different chemistry and mineral make-up, each magma differs in how easily it flows when coming out of a volcano. The colour of the rock that forms when the magma crystallizes also differs.

....

geologist someone who studies minerals, rocks and soil
composition what something is made of and how it is formed

A man photographs a lava flow at Mount Etna in Sicily, Italy.

IGNEOUS ROCKS IDENTIFICATION CHART

Type of magma	felsic	intermediate	mafic	ultramafic
Temperatures	700°C–900°C 1,292°F–1,652°F	900°C–1,000°C 1,652°F–1,832°F	1,000°C–1,100°C 1,832°F–2,012°F	1,100°C–1,200°C 2,012°F–2,192°F
Typical colours	white, pink, red	grey	dark grey, black	green
Type of mineral	Orthoclase · Quartz · Plagioclase · Pyroxene · Micas · Olivine · Amphibole			
Texture	Rock names			
Coarse-grained	granite	diorite	gabbro	peridotite
Fine-grained	rhyolite	andesite	basalt	

Mafic rocks are found at the top of Bowen's reaction series. Mafic magma is rich in calcium, iron and magnesium. These elements give minerals in mafic rocks a dark colour. Basalt is a fine-grained rock formed from mafic magma. Gabbro is an example of a coarse-grained rock formed from mafic magma.

At the bottom of Bowen's reaction series are felsic rocks. Felsic magmas are rich in silicate and feldspar. Felsic magma is thicker than mafic magma, and the rocks it forms are usually light in colour. These rocks make up the continents. Both volcanic and plutonic igneous rocks can form from felsic magmas.

Intermediate magma has a chemical make-up between that of mafic and felsic. The rocks it produces have some characteristics of both mafic and felsic rocks. Intermediate igneous rocks can be classified as high- or low-intermediate. High-intermediate rocks form at higher temperatures than low-intermediate rocks. Low-intermediate rocks have more quartz present than high-intermediate rocks.

Ultramafic magma is different from the other three types. Unlike mafic, intermediate or felsic magma, ultramafic magma does not contain any feldspar. It also contains less silicate than other types of magma, but it is rich in minerals such as olivine and pyroxene.

Komatiite is a rare volcanic rock of ultramafic origin. The rock features large olivine crystals.

diorite

pegmatite

granodiorite

SLOW-COOLING PLUTONIC ROCKS

Plutonic (intrusive) rocks can be felsic, intermediate or mafic. Gabbro is a mafic plutonic rock that is related to basalt. It has dark colours that range from dark green-grey to black. Because it is slow-cooling, it has large, coarse crystals.

Diorite is a high-intermediate plutonic rock. It is a very hard type of rock. Because the mix of minerals is black and white, the rock has a salt-and-pepper look. Diorite is similar to andesite (see page 22), but it is slow-cooling and has larger grains.

Pegmatite is one of the last rocks to form from slowly cooling magma. As a result, the crystals in pegmatite form at relatively low temperatures. Pegmatite contains large amounts of water vapour and fluorine gas. When the gas escapes, it leaves pockets in the pegmatite where beautiful gems such as topaz and garnet form.

Massive granite mountains make up the Tracy Arm Fjord in Alaska, USA.

Granite is a common type of rock on continents made by plutonic magma. Granite is a felsic rock that contains quartz, feldspar and mica. These rocks contain very little of the darker mafic minerals, which is why they are so light in colour. The slow-cooling minerals in granite form large crystals, which are easy to see. The crystals can be different colours, from black and light grey to white and pink. Granite is a very hard rock. Many mountains are made of granite and other intermediate and felsic rocks.

andesite

rhyolite

Fast-cooling volcanic rocks

Volcanic (extrusive) rocks can also be mafic, intermediate or felsic. Basalts are the most common type of igneous rock that cools fast from volcanic magma. Basalts are mafic rocks. As lava, basalts flow out quickly. Their appearance depends on how the lava cooled. Some basalts look like sponges because escaping gas in the magma created many holes. Others look like **pleated** cloth or bread dough because the pahoehoe lava wrinkled up in folds as it flowed out of the vent. Most basalts are black, but some are dark grey, red, brown or even green.

Andesite is an intermediate volcanic rock. As lava, andesite is very thick. It often explodes out of volcanoes in huge grey clouds and forms pyroclastic flows.

FACT

Hawaii has several beaches of black sand. They were created by water breaking down basalt that hardened from lava.

VERY FAST-COOLING ROCKS

Scoria is a very fast-cooling rock that is like glass. Scoria can come from either mafic or intermediate lava. Gases trapped in the lava create large holes in the rock.

scoria

Obsidian is a natural glass. It is created by lava that cools very fast. It cools so fast that crystals do not have time to form. Instead, the lava becomes a smooth, natural glass that is usually black. It contains elements that give it a dark colour. However, obsidian is a felsic rock that is closely related to two light-coloured rocks – slow-cooling granite and fast-cooling rhyolite.

obsidian

CHAPTER 4

FINDING IGNEOUS ROCKS

Igneous rocks are found all over Earth. Granite, diorite and granodiorite make up the base of continents. They are often found deep below Earth's surface. In the western United States, the Sierra Nevada range is made up of granite. New Hampshire, USA, is known as the Granite State because so much of its natural features are made up of dark grey granite. Pikes Peak in Colorado, USA, is known for its pink granite. Mount Rushmore is a famous US national monument in South Dakota. To create the monument, the faces of four US presidents were carved out of granite mountains.

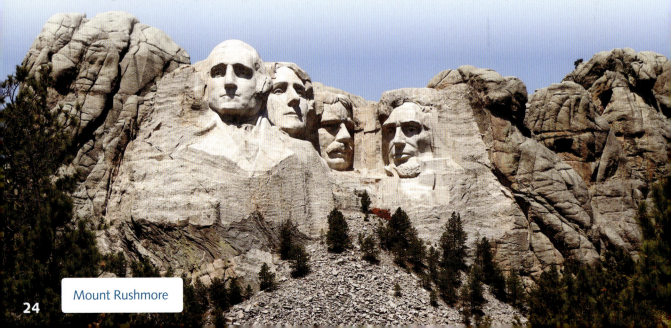

Mount Rushmore

MOUNT RUSHMORE

Artist Gutzon Borglum designed Mount Rushmore. It took 14 years and 400 workers to complete. Carvers, pointers, drillers and powdermen were all needed to create Borglum's design in the granite mountainside.

Pointers did all of the preparation work for the monument. They measured and marked the mountain so it could be drilled, blasted and carved. Pointers used a special machine invented by Borglum called a pointing machine. This helped the workers determine the measurements needed for the monument. They then attached themselves to a rope and harness and climbed over the cliff. The pointers marked the mountain with red paint for the drillers.

Next, the drillers got into special chairs called bosuns, also invented by Borglum. Once seated, the drillers were lowered over the edge to the red marks. With pneumatic drills, they drilled into the mountain in a honeycomb pattern of rows and columns.

The holes created by the drillers were used by powdermen. The powdermen carefully placed dynamite into the holes. The dynamite was cut to different lengths depending on how big a blast was needed.

Once ignited, huge chunks of rock were blown off the mountain and tumbled down into a pile below. Ninety per cent of the monument was created using dynamite.

Lastly, the carvers went to work. They used special tools to chisel and smooth the faces until they looked like stone skin. Borglum himself worked with the carvers. He wanted the monument to be perfect. The monument was completed in 1940. It features the faces of George Washington, Thomas Jefferson, Theodore Roosevelt and Abraham Lincoln.

Carvers work on the 20-metre (66-foot) granite sculpture of Abraham Lincoln's head.

While granite seems to be the most common igneous rock of the continents, basalt is the most common igneous rock of the oceans. Almost the entire ocean floor is made up of basalt. This igneous rock is constantly being formed along underwater cracks in Earth's crust. The ocean floor contains some of Earth's youngest rock.

There are more than 1,500 active land volcanoes on Earth and another 10,000 volcanoes on the ocean floor. There are also many dormant and extinct volcanoes, which have lots of igneous rocks. At Hawaii Volcanoes National Park, in the United States, tourists can visit active volcanoes. They can drive into a volcano's crater and see from a distance how the hot red lava cools and hardens into igneous rocks.

FACT

The entire rim of the Pacific Ocean is lined with volcanoes. This area is known as the Ring of Fire.

A tourist in Hawaii photographs a lava flow.

One famous place where igneous rocks exist in an unusual formation is the Giant's Causeway in Northern Ireland. The Giant's Causeway is found along the coast and is so-called because it looks like a road that giants may have walked along. Thousands of tall, six-sided columns are squeezed next to each other along this "roadway". This rock formation is made out of basalt and is called columnar lava. It formed when a sheet of lava cooled and then shrank and cracked into long vertical columns.

Tourists walk on the basalt columns at the Giant's Causeway in Northern Ireland.

CHAPTER 5

USES FOR IGNEOUS ROCKS

Igneous rocks are used for many purposes. On volcanic islands, people use the hard, dense volcanic rock to build houses and construct walls. Cinders are lightweight igneous rocks that are red, brown or black in colour. These rocks are often ground into smaller pieces and used like gravel to cover the surface of roads and paths.

Although granite is not the only type of stone used inside houses, it has become increasingly popular. Many people use granite for their worktops in kitchens and bathrooms. They like all of the colour variations found in its surface. They also appreciate its **durability** because it is such a hard rock.

durability able to last a long time

Igneous rocks are also used in jewellery. Obsidian looks like shiny, black glass. It can be cut and polished to make earrings, bracelets and necklaces. Peridot is a shiny green stone often used in rings and necklaces. Tourmaline, garnets and emeralds are all gemstones that form in the intrusive igneous rock pegmatite.

The use of igneous rocks is not new. People have used these rocks since ancient times. Stonehenge, in England, is an ancient stone circle made out of the igneous rock dolerite and the sedimentary rock sandstone. In ancient Mexico, people used obsidian to make arrowheads, knives and other types of weapons. Obsidian is still used in cutting instruments today. The blades of surgical scalpels are often made out of obsidian.

Stonehenge

GLOSSARY

basalt hard, dark rock made from cooled lava

composition what something is made of and how it is formed

crystal solid substance having a regular pattern of many flat surfaces

durability able to last a long time

fossil remains of an ancient plant or animal that have hardened into rock; also the preserved tracks or outline of an ancient organism

geologist someone who studies minerals, rocks and soil

pleat special type of fold

pyroclastic magma containing large amounts of gas that blasts out of a volcano in clouds of ash and rock

subduction zone place where the edge of one tectonic plate sinks beneath another

tectonic plate gigantic slab of Earth's crust that moves around on magma

FIND OUT MORE

BOOKS

Crystal and Gem (Eyewitness), DK (DK Children, 2014)

Igneous Rocks (Let's Rock), Chris Oxlade (Raintree, 2012)

Minerals (Rock On!), Chris Oxlade (Raintree, 2017)

Rock and Mineral (Eyewitness), DK (DK Children, 2014)

Volcanoes (DKfindout!), DK (DK Children, 2016)

WEBSITES

Learn more about rocks and soil.
www.bbc.co.uk/bitesize/ks2/science/materials/rocks_soils/read/1

Find out more about how igneous rocks are formed, and take the igneous rocks quiz!
www.dkfindout.com/uk/earth/rocks-and-minerals/how-are-igneous-rocks-formed

COMPREHENSION QUESTIONS

1. Describe two ways to group igneous rocks.

2. Igneous rocks are found all over Earth. What are some ways in which people have used igneous rocks?

3. What are two characteristics of mafic magma?

INDEX